Trust to Thrive

Building Relationships that Drive Sales

Written By Ross Kane

Copyright © 2024 Ross Kane

All rights reserved. No part of this publication may be reproduced, distributed, or transmitted in any form or by any means, including photocopying, recording, or other electronic or mechanical methods, without the prior written permission of the publisher, except in the case of brief quotations embodied in critical reviews and certain other noncommercial uses permitted by copyright law.

Table of Contents

INTRODUCTION

Why Trust Matters in Sales
    Importance of Trust in Business Relationships
    How Trust Affects Customer Loyalty and Sales

CHAPTER 1: UNDERSTANDING TRUST.

Define Trust in a Sales Context
    Trust Has Four Components: Reliability, Competence, Integrity, And Empathy.
    Trust Vs. Credibility

CHAPTER 2: DEVELOPING PERSONAL CREDIBILITY

Self-awareness and Honesty
    Authenticity In Sales Interactions.
    The Importance of Personal Integrity

Professionalism and Expertise.
    Continuous Learning and Staying Informed
    Sharing Knowledge Without Overselling.

CHAPTER 3: EFFECTIVE COMMUNICATION.

Active Listening.
    Techniques for Active Listening
    Demonstrating Genuine Interest In The Customer's Needs.

Clear and Transparent Communication.
    Being Open About Products/Services
    Setting realistic expectations.

CHAPTER 4: DELIVERING ON PROMISES

Consistency and Reliability
   Meeting Deadlines and Following Through
   Addressing Issues Quickly and Effectively

Building Trust Through Consistency and Reliability
   Practical Strategies for Consistency and Reliability

CHAPTER 5: BUILDING LONG-TERM RELATIONSHIPS

Beyond the Transaction
   Providing Value Beyond the Initial Sale
   Follow-up and Maintaining Contact

Customer Service Excellence
   Creating memorable customer experiences.
   Handling Complaints and Feedback constructively.

CHAPTER 6: LEVERAGING SOCIAL PROOF

Testimonials and Case Studies
   Collecting and Using Customer Testimonials
   Creating Compelling Case Studies.

Creating an Online Presence
   Using Social Media to Increase Trust
   Engaging with Customers Online

CHAPTER 7: ETHICAL SELLING PRACTICES

Avoid Manipulative Tactics.
   Ethical Persuasion vs. Manipulation

Transparency in Pricing and Policies
   Clear Pricing Structures
   Transparent Return and Refund Policies

CHAPTER 8: ADAPTING TO DIFFERENT PERSONALITIES

Understanding Customers' Personalities
    Adapting Sales Strategies for Different Personality Types
    Establishing Rapport with Various Customer Types

CONCLUSION

Introduction

Why Trust Matters in Sales

In the domain of sales, trust is more than a simple buzzword, it's the cornerstone upon which durable commercial relationships are established. While techniques, plans, and skills play significant roles in sales, trust stands out as the solitary characteristic that consistently predicts long-term success. Trust drives every stage of the sales process, from the initial contact to the final transaction and beyond. This introduction delves into why trust matters in sales, demonstrating its significance in corporate relationships and its tremendous impact on client loyalty and sales.

Importance of Trust in Business Relationships

Trust is the foundation of all meaningful relationships, whether personal and professional. In the context of sales, trust means that customers believe in the salesperson's capacity to deliver on promises, operate with integrity, and prioritize their best interests. This mindset converts a transactional contact into a partnership that encourages mutual respect and loyalty.

Building Credibility: Trust begins with credibility. For sales professionals, creating credibility entails demonstrating product knowledge, industry competence, and a true grasp of the customer's demands. Credibility is created over time through consistent, reliable, and honest interactions. When clients see a salesperson as credible, they are more inclined to engage in meaningful conversations and consider their advice seriously.

Enhancing conversation: Trust enables open and honest conversation. Customers who trust a salesman are more inclined to communicate their actual requirements, preferences, and concerns. This transparency enables the salesperson to adjust their approach, providing solutions that are more closely matched with the customer's individual needs. As a result, this individualized approach can considerably increase the value provided to the consumer.

Reducing Perceived Risk: Purchasing decisions are intrinsically risky. Customers frequently assess the possible benefits of a product or service against the perceived risks of making the wrong choice. Trust decreases perceived risk by reassuring customers that they are making a safe and informed decision. When clients believe that a salesperson has their best interests at heart, they are more confidence in their purchasing decisions, resulting in smoother transactions and fewer complaints.

Trust is an important driver of long-term engagement. Customers who trust a salesperson or a business are more inclined to make repeat purchases. This ongoing relationship not only increases repeat business, but it also encourages clients to explore the company's other products or services. Long-term involvement benefits both parties by building loyalty and stability.

Creating Brand champions: Trust may turn delighted customers into ardent brand champions. Customers who have positive, trust-building interactions with salespeople are more inclined to promote the company to others. This word-of-mouth promotion is extremely beneficial, as suggestions from reliable sources are typically more persuasive than formal advertising. Brand supporters may greatly improve a company's reputation and increase its client base.

How Trust Affects Customer Loyalty and Sales

The importance of trust for client loyalty and revenue cannot be emphasized. Trust is a key motivator for customer behavior, influencing both their purchasing decisions and their overall relationship with the brand.

Fostering Customer Loyalty: Customer loyalty is built on trust. Customers who trust a company are more likely to stay loyal, especially when faced with competing offers. This loyalty leads to repeat business, which is essential for continuous revenue development. Loyal consumers are also less price-sensitive, prioritizing the relationship and consistent quality over the possible cost savings of switching to a competitor.

Trust increases the lifetime worth of a consumer. A trusting connection helps clients to make repeat purchases, try new products or services, and sign long-term contracts. Increased customer lifetime value (CLV) is an important indicator for any organization since it represents the total revenue that can be expected from a single client over the course of their relationship.

Increasing Sales with Referrals: Trust-driven loyalty leads to referrals, which are a highly effective method of acquiring new customers. Customers that are satisfied and loyal to a company are more inclined to suggest it to their friends, family, and coworkers. These referrals frequently produce high-quality leads since potential customers are more likely to believe the suggestions of their peers.

Enhancing Customer Retention: Customer retention is heavily driven by trust. Companies that prioritize creating and sustaining trust are more likely to keep their consumers for the long run. Retaining clients is frequently more cost-effective than obtaining new ones since it needs less marketing and sales investment. High retention rates help to stabilize revenue streams and reduce client churn.

Trust also plays an important role in upselling and cross-selling. Customers who trust a firm are more willing to try new products or services. They trust the company's advice and are eager to spend in solutions they see as useful. Effective upselling and cross-selling can considerably boost average transaction value and overall sales revenue.

Strengthening Brand Reputation: Trust improves a company's reputation. A solid, trust-based reputation attracts new clients and retains existing ones. In the age of social media and online evaluations, a good reputation can provide a major competitive advantage. Customers are more willing to interact with firms that have been repeatedly complimented for their integrity and dependability.

Finally, trust is an essential component of the sales process. It supports all effective corporate relationships by increasing client loyalty, improving communication, and lowering perceived risk. Trust not only boosts sales and revenue, but it also encourages long-term involvement and brand loyalty. Prioritizing trust-building activities is critical for both sales people and firms seeking long-term success and growth.

This book seeks to deliver the ideas, techniques, and resources required to create trust and harness its power in today's competitive sales landscape.

Chapter 1: Understanding Trust.

Trust is the foundation of all successful sales relationships. It establishes the foundation for long-term client loyalty and recurring business. Understanding the subtleties of trust in a sales context is crucial for any sales professional looking to develop long-term and meaningful connections with their customers. This chapter defines trust in sales, discusses the major components that make it up, and distinguishes between trust and credibility.

Define Trust in a Sales Context

In sales, trust is described as the customer's confidence in the salesperson's dependability, skill, honesty, and empathy. It is the assurance that the salesman would operate in the customer's best interests, keep promises, and add value. Trust is more than just making a sale; it is about building a connection that can weather time and adversity, generating customer loyalty and repeat business.

Trust Has Four Components: Reliability, Competence, Integrity, And Empathy.

Reliability in sales refers to continuously delivering on commitments and meeting or exceeding client expectations. It entails being dependable and following through on your promises. This could be as easy as returning a phone call as promised or delivering a product on time. Reliability fosters trust by showing the customer that they can rely on the salesperson and the firm.

Competence is defined as the capacity to display the knowledge, skills, and expertise required to effectively satisfy the needs of the client. It entails being knowledgeable about your product or service, understanding the market, and being able to make intelligent recommendations. A skilled salesperson can correctly answer questions, provide valuable insights, and solve problems efficiently. Competence reassures clients that they are working with a professional who can assist them in achieving their goals.

Integrity means being honest and ethical in all relationships. It entails being open about what your product or service can and cannot do, admitting mistakes when they arise, and avoiding dishonest techniques. Integrity fosters trust by demonstrating that the salesman is principled and dedicated to doing the right thing, even if it means losing a sale in the short term. Customers admire honesty and are more inclined to stay loyal to a company that performs ethically.

Empathy is the understanding and sharing of your customers' experiences and opinions. It entails actively listening, expressing genuine concern for their wants and issues, and reacting in a manner that shows you care. Empathy helps to establish a connection with customers, making them feel appreciated and understood. An empathic salesman can adjust their approach to each customer's individual demands, improving the entire experience.

Trust Vs. Credibility

While trust and credibility are closely related, they are not identical. Credibility is the perception that a salesman is believable and trustworthy based on their experience and track record. Trust, on the other hand, is a more deeply felt conviction in the salesperson's dependability, integrity, and intent.

Credibility is frequently the first step in developing trust. It is built on knowledge, expertise, and the capacity to produce outcomes. A competent salesperson has a demonstrated track record, credentials, and the experience required to give value to customers. They communicate with authority, supported by facts and experience, reassuring the buyer of their abilities. Credibility can be developed by delivering factual information, exhibiting expertise, and highlighting previous triumphs.

Trust extends beyond credibility and includes the emotional and relational aspects of the sales connection. Credibility is believing in a salesperson's ability, whereas trust is believing in their character and intentions. Trust develops over time through continuous, good interactions that exhibit dependability, honesty, and empathy. It needs the salesperson to be not just knowledgeable, but also sincerely concerned about the customer's well-being.

In essence, credibility is the antecedent of trust. A salesperson may be believable, but unless they demonstrate honesty and empathy, they can never totally earn the customer's trust. A salesperson who earns trust by being dependable, skilled, and empathic will be perceived as credible.

- **Building Trust in Sales**

Building trust in sales involves a conscious and consistent effort across all customer contacts. Here are some important ways for developing trust:

Consistency in action and communication is essential. Customers must see that you are consistent and predictable in your behavior. Deliver on your promises, be punctual, and follow up as needed.

Transparency: Be open and honest in all interactions. Provide specific information about your products and services, including any restrictions or potential problems. Transparency increases credibility and creates confidence.

Active Listening: Pay close attention to the consumer, acknowledge their concerns, and reply wisely. This conveys empathy and indicates that you value their input.

Maintain a high level of professionalism during all encounters. This means being prepared, competent, and respectful. Professionalism improves competence and credibility.

Building Relationships: Prioritize long-term relationships over fast sales. Show real concern for your customers' requirements and seek to be an important partner in their success.

Responsiveness: Respond quickly to consumer concerns and requests. Quick and effective problem solving indicates dependability and a dedication to customer pleasure.

Follow-Up: Contact clients on a regular basis to check their satisfaction and handle any ongoing requirements. Follow-ups demonstrate that you care about their experience after the first sale.

Chapter 2: Developing Personal Credibility

Building personal credibility is an important part of sales success. Credibility is the foundation of trust and is required for establishing and maintaining productive commercial relationships. This chapter will discuss the significance of self-awareness and honesty, as well as the role of professionalism and experience in building and maintaining personal credibility.

Self-awareness and Honesty

Authenticity In Sales Interactions.

Authenticity is the foundation for devcloping credibility in sales. Being authentic entails presenting oneself in a true and sincere manner, as opposed to constructing a persona geared primarily for closing business. Customers respond to authenticity, which fosters a sense of connection and trust that artificial or rehearsed encounters cannot create.

Understanding Personal Values: The first step toward authenticity is to understand one's own values, beliefs, and motives. Sales professionals who are clear about their values are more likely to speak consistently and authentically. This clarity aids in aligning personal actions with professional objectives, making every customer interaction more honest and impactful.

Being Transparent: Transparency is an essential component of authenticity. This entails being honest about a product or service's benefits and limitations rather than exaggerating its capabilities. Customers value honesty and are more inclined to trust salespeople who offer a balanced perspective, including any drawbacks. Transparency also entails being open about any mistakes or issues that arise, and accepting responsibility for fixing them.

Authentic sales professionals demonstrate consistent behavior throughout all conversations. Consistency fosters reliability, which is an essential component of trust. When customers know what to expect from a salesperson, they are more likely to engage favorably and feel at ease when completing a purchase.

Emotional Intelligence: Authenticity is inextricably tied to emotional intelligence, which includes being aware of and controlling one's own emotions, as well as understanding and influencing the emotions of others. Sales professionals with high emotional intelligence can better navigate complex customer interactions, fostering a culture of trust and mutual respect.

The Importance of Personal Integrity

Personal integrity is the persistent commitment to ethical principles and moral values. It is critical to establishing and sustaining confidence in sales. Sales professionals with high integrity are perceived as trustworthy and dependable, attributes that are essential in developing long-term business connections.

Ethical Decision-Making: Integrity entails making ethical decisions that are in the best interests of the client, even if they are not the most convenient or profitable option. Ethical decision-making necessitates a strong commitment to doing what is right, which fosters consumer trust and loyalty.

Honoring Commitments: Keeping pledges and commitments demonstrates personal integrity. When salespeople consistently deliver on their commitments, it boosts their reputation. This includes being on time, fulfilling deadlines, and following through on agreements, all of which demonstrate reliability to the consumer.

Respecting Confidentiality: Salespeople frequently have access to sensitive information about their clients. Respecting and safeguarding this confidentiality is critical. Breaching secrecy can seriously undermine credibility and trust. On the other side, keeping confidentiality indicates respect and integrity, boosting the trust clients place in the salesperson.

Admitting Mistakes: Everyone makes mistakes, but how they are handled has a big impact on trustworthiness. Sales people who recognize their mistakes and take swift action to correct them show honesty. This willingness to be accountable and honest in challenging situations can increase trust since it demonstrates a dedication to the customer's best interests.

Professionalism and Expertise.
Continuous Learning and Staying Informed

Professionalism in sales is inextricably linked to expertise. Customers rely on sales experts not only to offer them a product, but also to assist them through difficult purchasing decisions with expert guidance and insights. Continuous learning and being informed are critical for maintaining and improving this competencc.

Industry Knowledge: Keeping up with industry trends, technical breakthroughs, and market shifts is critical. This understanding enables salespeople to deliver relevant and timely information to their consumers, establishing themselves as valued resources rather than simple sellers. Regularly reading business publications, attending conferences, and participating in professional networks are all good strategies to keep updated.

Product Mastery: Knowing the items or services being sold inside and out is critical. This includes understanding all features, benefits, restrictions, and potential applications. Product mastery helps salespeople to confidently answer inquiries, conduct extensive demonstrations, and address any concerns that customers may have. It also enables for more precise customisation of solutions to meet unique customer requirements.

Skill Development: Sales approaches and strategies evolve with time. Continuous skill development through training programs, workshops, and courses enables sales professionals to stay on top of their game. This continuing development may include improving communication skills, learning new sales approaches, or mastering digital sales tools and platforms.

Customer insights: Understanding customer behavior, preferences, and pain points is a continuous activity. To stay on top of their clients' changing needs, sales professionals should collect and analyze customer feedback, market research, and competitor analysis on a consistent basis. This customer-centric strategy not only increases credibility, but it also promotes deeper, more meaningful relationships.

Sharing Knowledge Without Overselling.

Sharing knowledge efficiently without overselling is a skill that distinguishes respectable sales people from others. It entails offering important insights and information that assist clients in making informed decisions, rather than forcing them to make a purchase.

Educational Approach: Using an educational approach entails establishing yourself as a consultant rather than a salesperson. Sales professionals can create trust and rapport with their customers by teaching them about the product or service, its benefits, and how it might meet their individual needs. This approach indicates a real interest in assisting the consumer, rather than simply closing a transaction.

Balanced Information: It is critical to provide a balanced assessment of a product or service that considers both its strengths and limitations. This clarity allows buyers to trust the sales professional's advise. Highlighting potential issues and how they might be mitigated demonstrates honesty and a thorough understanding of the products.

Listening and responding: Effective knowledge sharing begins with attentive listening. Understanding a customer's requirements, problems, and inquiries enables salespeople to give relevant and targeted information. Responding thoughtfully and completely to consumer inquiries builds trust and displays a willingness to address their individual issue.

Avoiding High-Pressure Sales: High-pressure sales tactics can undermine trust and credibility. Instead, salespeople should focus on providing a welcoming and encouraging environment in which consumers may explore their alternatives and make decisions at their own time. This method promotes a great consumer experience and long-term partnerships.

Using Testimonials and Case Studies: Sharing success stories, testimonials, and case studies can be a powerful approach to impart knowledge without overselling. These real-world examples show how the product or service has helped others in comparable situations, providing actual evidence of value. This strategy fosters trust by providing social proof and assisting clients in visualizing possible outcomes.

Building personal credibility is key for sales success. Self-awareness, honesty, professionalism, and knowledge are essential components in this process. Authenticity and personal integrity establish trust, while ongoing learning and educated knowledge sharing strengthen a sales professional's reputation. By focusing on these areas, salespeople can build trusting connections that lead to long-term success and client loyalty.

Chapter 3: Effective Communication.

Effective communication is the key to successful sales encounters. It entails not just speaking effectively, but also actively listening and transparently communicating information. Communication in sales is more than just exchanging words; it's about connecting with the consumer, understanding their needs, and building trust. This chapter delves into the ideas of active listening and clear, open communication, both of which are essential for building strong, trust-based relationships with clients.

Active Listening.

Active listening is a valuable weapon in the salesperson's arsenal. It entails fully interacting with the customer, understanding their requirements and problems, and responding wisely. Active listening goes beyond hearing words; it includes interpreting the underlying emotions and intentions behind those words.

Techniques for Active Listening

Paying Full Attention: The first step in active listening is giving the customer your undivided attention. This entails removing distractions, keeping eye contact, and focusing solely on what the consumer is saying. By being totally present, you demonstrate to the consumer that you appreciate their feedback and are committed to understanding their viewpoint.

Reflective Listening entails paraphrasing or summarizing what the consumer has stated to ensure comprehension. For example, you could say, "What I'm hearing is that you're searching for a solution that will work with your current systems. Is this correct?"This strategy not only clarifies the message, but it also demonstrates to the customer that you are actively engaged and trying to understand their needs.

Open-ended questions empower customers to provide more specific information about their requirements and concerns. Instead of answering yes-or-no questions, try asking questions that encourage elaboration, such as, "Can you tell me more about the difficulties you're experiencing with your present solution?"This technique encourages deeper interactions and delivers more information about the customer's position.

Empathizing with the consumer: Empathy is putting yourself in the shoes of the consumer and understanding their emotions and perspectives. Empathy may help you connect with a consumer and make them feel heard and respected. Statements such as "I understand why that would be frustrating," or "It sounds like you're under a lot of pressure," can help affirm the customer's feelings and deepen the relationship.

Nonverbal Communication: Active listening is being aware of nonverbal indicators, both yours and the customer's. Nod in agreement, smile when appropriate, and maintain an open posture to demonstrate that you are interested. Pay attention to the customer's body language, since it can reveal additional information about their thoughts and feelings.

Demonstrating Genuine Interest In The Customer's Needs.

Personalizing Interactions: Demonstrate real interest by personalizing your interactions to each individual customer. Use their name, refer to earlier interactions, and demonstrate that you remember and care about their particular circumstance. This personal touch can significantly impact how the customer perceives your involvement.

Demonstrating Knowledge and Understanding: To display genuine interest, you must grasp the customer's industry, difficulties, and objectives. This necessitates significant research and preparation before to meetings. Customers are more likely to perceive you as a helpful partner who genuinely cares about their achievement if you can speak intelligently about their situation.

Following Up Thoughtfully: After the initial chat, provide the consumer with pertinent information, resources, or solutions that answer their needs. This follow-up demonstrates that you were attentive and devoted to assisting them in finding the best solution. Personalized follow-ups can also strengthen the bond and keep the conversation going.

Providing Value Beyond Sales: Demonstrate that your interest in the customer extends beyond the sale. Share your sector knowledge, offer to connect them with other specialists who can assist them, or provide relevant resources that address their concerns. This attitude communicates that you are committed to their achievement and see the connection as a long-term collaboration.

Clear and Transparent Communication.

Clear and open communication is critical for establishing trust and ensuring that customers have all of the information they require to make informed decisions. It entails being honest, straightforward, and avoiding misunderstandings or hidden surprises.

Being Open About Products/Services

Customers appreciate honesty about a product or service's capabilities and limitations. Clearly explaining the capabilities and limitations helps to set realistic expectations and prevent future disappointments. For example, if a product excels in some areas but lacks in others, make sure to communicate this openly. Honesty about limitations can boost credibility and trust.

Providing Comprehensive Information: Ensure that clients have all of the information they require to make informed selections. This includes detailed product specifications, usage instructions, pricing, and any possible additional costs. Comprehensive information makes customers feel more confident in their purchase and reduces the possibility of misunderstandings or dissatisfaction.

Highlighting Benefits and Drawbacks: While it is important to highlight the advantages of your product or service, it is also critical to discuss any potential drawbacks. Being open about both sides demonstrates transparency and allows customers to weigh their options more effectively. This balanced approach builds trust and shows that you have the customer's best interests at heart.

Clear Communication of Policies: Be open and honest about company policies regarding returns, warranties, and service agreements. Customers need to understand the terms and conditions of their purchase. Clear communication of these policies helps to prevent future conflicts and establishes a foundation of trust.

Setting realistic expectations.

Avoiding Overpromising: Overpromising and underdelivering is a quick way to lose trust. It is critical to establish reasonable expectations for what your product or service can achieve. Be upfront about timetables, potential problems, and the outcomes that customers can anticipate. Underpromising and overdelivering is a method for building credibility and exceeding client expectations.

Providing Accurate timetables: Clear and accurate communication about timetables is critical. Customers should know what to expect when a product is delivered, a service is implemented, or a problem is resolved. If delays occur, tell them quickly and provide updates. This transparency helps to manage expectations and exhibit dependability.

Clarifying Roles and obligations: In complex sales or service agreements, it is critical to define the roles and obligations of both parties. Customers should understand what is necessary on their end for successful deployment and what they may expect from you. Clear definition of responsibilities helps to avoid misunderstandings and promotes smooth communication.

Addressing Potential obstacles Upfront: Discuss any potential obstacles or issues that may occur and how they will be addressed. Preparing clients for potential barriers indicates forethought and proactive behavior. It also reassures customers that you are prepared to assist them throughout the process, which increases trust.

Consistent Follow-Up and Communication: Maintain consistent follow-up and communication throughout the sales process and after the sale is completed. Regular updates, progress reports, and check-ins show that you are committed to the customer's satisfaction and success. This ongoing communication helps reinforce trust and keeps the relationship strong.

Effective communication in sales hinges on the principles of active listening and clear, transparent communication. Active listening involves engaging fully with the customer, understanding their needs, and responding thoughtfully. Techniques including as paying complete attention, contemplative listening, asking open-ended questions, and displaying empathy are vital for demonstrating genuine interest in the customer's demands. Clear and honest communication requires being upfront about product capabilities and limitations, offering thorough information, highlighting both benefits and drawbacks, and setting realistic expectations. By mastering these communication tactics, sales professionals may develop strong, trust-based relationships with their consumers, leading to long-term success and loyalty.

Chapter 4: Delivering on Promises

Delivering on promises is a cornerstone of building trust in any business relationship. In sales, the ability to regularly honor commitments and address difficulties swiftly and effectively can considerably boost a salesperson's reputation and promote long-term customer loyalty. This chapter will discuss the importance of consistency and reliability, focusing on fulfilling deadlines, following through on pledges, and addressing difficulties with speed and efficiency.

Consistency and Reliability

Consistency and reliability are fundamental qualities that customers seek in their interactions with sales professionals. These traits demonstrate that a salesperson is dependable, trustworthy, and capable of delivering on promises.

Meeting Deadlines and Following Through

Establishing Realistic Timelines: Setting realistic timelines is the first step in ensuring that commitments are met. Sales professionals must assess their capacity and resources accurately before committing to a deadline. Overpromising can lead to missed deadlines, which damages credibility and trust. It's better to set conservative estimates and exceed expectations than to fall short of an ambitious promise.

Clear Communication of Deadlines: Once a schedule is defined, it's vital to convey it effectively to all stakeholders. Customers should be informed about when they may expect deliverables, and any internal teams engaged should understand their duties and timeframes. Clear communication helps manage expectations and ensures that everyone is aligned and working towards the same goals.

Creating a System for Tracking Progress: Effective project management entails tracking progress against defined deadlines. Sales personnel should use tools and systems that allow them to track tasks, milestones, and deliveries.

Regularly updating these tools helps in spotting potential delays early and taking corrective action to stay on track.

Prioritizing Tasks: To meet deadlines consistently, sales professionals must prioritize tasks based on their importance and urgency. Critical tasks that directly impact the customer should be given priority to ensure that key deliverables are met on time. Effective prioritization helps in managing workload and maintaining focus on what matters most.

Regular Status Updates: Providing regular status updates to customers keeps them informed about the progress of their orders or projects. Even if everything is on track, updates reassure customers that their needs are being addressed. In the event of any delays or adjustments, early communication aids in managing expectations and collectively developing solutions.

Commitment to Follow Through: Following through on commitments entails seeing tasks through to completion. Sales professionals must ensure that all promised actions are carried out and that deliverables are delivered as agreed. This follow-through demonstrates dependability and builds trust with customers, demonstrating that the salesperson is trustworthy and committed to their success.

Addressing Issues Quickly and Effectively

Proactive Issue Identification: Being able to recognize potential difficulties before they become problems is an important talent in sales. Sales people can identify warning indicators early by constantly reviewing the status of orders and initiatives. Proactive issue identification enables timely intervention, reducing the impact on the customer while maintaining trust.

Quick Problem Resolution: When problems develop, it is critical to respond quickly. Customers want problems to be addressed quickly and with haste. An immediate acknowledgement of the problem, followed by prompt action to remedy it, indicates a dedication to client satisfaction and dependability.

Effective Problem-Solving Skills: Strong problem-solving abilities are required for effective issue resolution.

Salespeople should be able to examine a situation, determine the root cause, and implement solutions that address the issue completely. Involving relevant stakeholders and leveraging available resources can aid in the development of effective and long-term solutions.

Transparency is essential when dealing with problems. Customers should be kept informed about the nature of the issue, the steps being taken to resolve it, and the expected timeline for resolution. Transparent communication helps manage customer expectations and reassures them that their concerns are being taken seriously.

Learning from Mistakes: Every issue provides an opportunity to learn and improve. After resolving a problem, it's important to conduct a post-mortem analysis to understand what went wrong and how similar issues can be prevented in the future. Implementing changes based on these insights helps in enhancing processes and reducing the likelihood of recurring problems.

Empathy and Customer Support: Addressing issues effectively also involves showing empathy and providing robust customer support. Sales professionals should acknowledge the inconvenience caused to the customer and offer sincere apologies. Providing support throughout the resolution process helps in maintaining a positive customer experience despite the challenges.

Building Trust Through Consistency and Reliability

Establishing a Reputation for Dependability: Consistency in meeting deadlines and following through on commitments helps in building a reputation for dependability. Customers come to rely on sales professionals who consistently deliver as promised, which strengthens the relationship and fosters loyalty.

Creating Positive Customer Experiences: Delivering on promises contributes to positive customer experiences. When customers receive what they expect, when they expect it, their overall satisfaction with the sales process increases. Positive experiences encourage repeat business and referrals, which are vital for long-term success.

Enhancing Customer Loyalty: Reliability and consistency are key drivers of customer loyalty. Customers are more likely to remain loyal to sales professionals and organizations that consistently meet their demands and address issues immediately. Loyal customers are valuable assets, providing ongoing business and acting as advocates for the brand.

Building Long-Term Relationships: Trust is the foundation of long-term commercial relationships. By consistently delivering on promises and effectively addressing issues, sales professionals can build strong, enduring relationships with their customers. These relationships are mutually beneficial, giving stability and growth opportunities for both parties.

Increasing Customer Referrals: Satisfied consumers are more inclined to refer others to sales experts they trust. Word-of-mouth referrals are a major source of new business and are generally founded on a reputation for reliability and consistency. By delivering on commitments, sales professionals can generate favorable word-of-mouth and extend their customer base.

Supporting Brand Reputation: Consistent delivery and excellent issue resolution contribute to a good brand reputation. A brand known for reliability and customer satisfaction draws more business and stands out in a competitive market. Sales professionals play a critical role in keeping and strengthening this image through their contacts with clients.

Practical Strategies for Consistency and Reliability

Developing Standard Operating Procedures: Establishing standard operating procedures (SOPs) for common tasks ensures consistency in how these tasks are performed. SOPs provide clear guidelines and best practices, reducing variability and increasing reliability in service delivery.

Utilizing Technology for Efficiency: Leveraging technology can enhance efficiency and reliability. CRM systems, project management tools, and communication platforms help in tracking tasks, managing customer interactions, and ensuring that deadlines are met. Technology also facilitates transparent communication and issue tracking.

Training and Development: Ongoing training and development for sales professionals ensure that they have the skills and knowledge needed to deliver consistently. Training should cover time management, communication, problem-solving, and customer service. Continuous learning aids in maintaining high levels of performance.

Setting Clear Expectations with Customers: From the start, it is critical to establish clear expectations with customers regarding timelines, deliverables, and potential challenges. Clear expectations help to avoid misunderstandings and ensure that customers know what to expect, which reduces the likelihood of dissatisfaction.

Regular Performance Reviews: Conducting regular performance reviews assists in identifying areas for improvement and celebrating accomplishments. These evaluations should analyze the sales professional's ability to meet deadlines, follow through on commitments, and effectively resolve concerns. The feedback from these reviews can help guide professional development and process improvements.

Cultivating a Customer-Centric Culture: A customer-centric culture puts the demands and satisfaction of customers first. Sales people should be taught to view every engagement through the customer's eyes and strive to exceed their expectations. Cultivating this culture guarantees that keeping promises is a key priority.

Delivering on promises with consistency and dependability is critical for establishing trust and developing strong customer relationships in sales. Sales professionals can improve their credibility, create positive customer experiences, and build a loyal customer base by meeting deadlines, following through on commitments, and responding to issues quickly and effectively. Practical strategies such as developing SOPs, utilizing technology, continuous training, and setting clear expectations support these efforts. Ultimately, the ability to deliver on promises distinguishes successful sales professionals and contributes significantly to long-term business success.

Chapter 5: Building Long-Term Relationships

In the realm of sales, fostering long-term relationships with customers is far more valuable than focusing solely on individual transactions. Establishing lasting relationships involves going beyond the initial sale to provide ongoing value and exceptional customer service. This chapter explores strategies for offering value beyond the transaction, maintaining consistent follow-ups, and delivering customer service excellence, including creating memorable experiences and handling complaints constructively.

Beyond the Transaction

Providing Value Beyond the Initial Sale

Building long-term relationships with customers requires a commitment to providing ongoing value well after the initial sale. This continuous engagement helps to reinforce the customer's decision to choose your product or service and encourages loyalty.

Offering Continuous Support and Resources: Customers appreciate continuing support that helps them maximize the benefits of their purchase. This can include regular check-ins to see how they are using the product, sharing recommendations and best practices, and providing additional resources such as guides, webinars, or training sessions. Continuous support ensures that consumers feel appreciated and supported throughout their journey.

Sharing Industry Insights and Updates: Informing customers on industry trends, new technology, and market developments establishes you as a valued resource. Regularly offering important articles, studies, and insights keeps consumers informed and indicates your dedication to their success. This proactive approach promotes a stronger connection and supports your role as a trusted counsel.

Personalizing follow-up interactions based on the customer's personal requirements and preferences demonstrates your understanding and concern for their unique circumstance. Tailored follow-ups can address specific difficulties, provide new products or services that may be useful, and provide unique solutions that improve customer experience.

Implementing client Loyalty Programs: Loyalty programs that reward repeat customers with discounts, exclusive offers, or exclusive services can help increase client retention. These programs thank customers for their continued business and offer additional incentives to keep the relationship going. They also provide opportunities for additional engagement and value delivery.

Soliciting and Responding to Feedback: Actively seeking consumer feedback on their experience and the product or service they received is critical for continual improvement. Responding to this input displays that you value their thoughts and are devoted to satisfying their requirements. Implementing adjustments based on consumer feedback can result in improved products and services, creating more loyalty.

Follow-up and Maintaining Contact

Consistent follow-up and regular communication are vital for developing long-term consumer connections. These conversations help to maintain the relationship and guarantee that consumers continue to feel supported and valued.

Schedule regular check-ins to discuss how the consumer is using your product or service. These check-ins can be informal and conversational, focusing on their experiences and any extra needs they might have. Regular touchpoints help preserve the relationship and create opportunity to offer further support.

Tailored Communication: Use tailored communication to stay connected with clients. Tailor your messaging depending on their previous interactions, preferences, and comments. Personalized emails, phone calls, or even handwritten notes may make clients feel special and valued.

Automating Follow-Ups with a Personal Touch: While automation can help handle follow-ups efficiently, it's crucial to keep a personal touch. Automated emails and messages should be personalized to include the customer's name and reference their individual situation or purchasing history. This strategy blends efficiency with a personalized feel, keeping the relationship warm.

Unique Occasion Outreach: Acknowledge and celebrate unique occasions with your clients, such as anniversaries of their purchase, birthdays, or accomplishments in their business. Sending greetings or modest presents of thanks on these occasions indicates thoughtfulness and deepens the personal connection.

Providing Value in Each Interaction: Ensure that each follow-up interaction gives some type of value to the consumer. This could be through sharing important information, offering support, or simply checking in to indicate that you care. Value-driven interactions improve the relationship and keep customers engaged.

Customer Service Excellence

Creating memorable customer experiences.

Delivering exceptional customer service is crucial to creating memorable experiences that promote long-term loyalty. Exceptional service goes beyond meeting basic expectations to delighting consumers and creating a lasting favorable impression.

Personalized Service: Tailoring your service to the particular needs and preferences of each consumer produces a personalized experience. This could involve tailoring product suggestions, delivering unique solutions, or providing bespoke assistance. Personalized service makes customers feel cherished and understood.

Anticipating Customer demands: Exceptional customer service entails anticipating client demands before they are addressed. By identifying their routines, preferences, and prospective problem points, you can proactively offer solutions and support. This foresight indicates a strong grasp of the customer and enriches their overall experience.

Delivering Consistent Quality: Consistency in service quality is vital for developing confidence and reliability. Ensure that every engagement, whether it's through sales, support, or follow-ups, maintains a high degree of excellence. Consistency maintains the customer's faith in your brand and encourages repeat business.

Going the Extra Mile: Small gestures that go above and beyond basic service can create memorable experiences. This might include quicker service for urgent requirements, thoughtful gestures such as complementary improvements, or addressing concerns in a way that exceeds expectations. Going the extra mile shows that you truly care about the customer's satisfaction.

Creating Positive Touchpoints: Each interaction with a consumer presents an opportunity to establish a positive touchpoint. From the first contact to after-sales assistance, make sure that every touchpoint is geared to improve the customer's experience. Positive touchpoints aggregate over time, resulting in a strong, favorable perception of your brand.

Handling Complaints and Feedback constructively.

Handling complaints and feedback constructively is critical to sustaining and improving long-term partnerships. How you respond to and resolve issues has a huge impact on client happiness and loyalty.

Listening Actively and Empathetically: When consumers make complaints, it is critical to listen actively and empathetically. Understand their issues completely and recognize their emotions. Empathy demonstrates that you care about their situation and are determined to resolve the problem.

Respond to complaints quickly and transparently. Customers may get even more frustrated if responses are delayed or ambiguous. Provide specific information about the efforts you're taking to resolve the issue, and keep the client updated throughout the process.

Taking Ownership and Responsibility: Accept responsibility for any errors or shortcomings that contributed to the complaint. Taking ownership displays accountability and a desire to fix the situation.

Implementing Effective Solutions: Make sure that the solutions you supply effectively meet the customer's concerns. This could include replacing a broken product, issuing a refund, or giving more help. Effective solutions reflect a commitment to client satisfaction and can transform a bad experience into a good one.

Following Up After Resolution: After resolving a complaint, communicate with the customer to confirm their satisfaction. This follow-up demonstrates that you are really concerned about their experience and want to ensure that the problem has been completely resolved. It also provides an opportunity to obtain further input and strengthen the relationship.

Learning from comments: View complaints and comments as wonderful chances to learn and develop. Analyze the underlying causes of problems and adopt solutions to avoid them from reoccurring. Continuous improvement based on client input helps you enhance your products, services, and overall customer experience.

Chapter 6: Leveraging Social Proof

In the digital age, social proof is an effective method for establishing trust and credibility in sales. Social proof, a psychological phenomena in which people make judgments based on the actions and opinions of others, can have a substantial impact on potential consumers' purchase behavior. This chapter discusses how to use testimonials and case studies effectively, as well as how to establish a strong online presence through social media, to increase customer trust and engagement.

Testimonials and Case Studies

Collecting and Using Customer Testimonials

Customer testimonials are among the most powerful types of social proof. They present real-life examples of customer pleasure and success, reassuring potential purchasers that your product or service lives up to its promises.

Encourage Satisfied Customers to Share Their Experiences: Proactively seek testimonials from satisfied customers. After a successful sale or a nice customer service interaction, invite customers to share their experiences. Simplify the process by giving them a template or a few leading questions to help them express their ideas. Personalized requests can lead to better responses because clients feel appreciated and recognized.

Highlighting Specific Benefits and Outcomes: Effective testimonials go beyond general appreciation to emphasize specific benefits and outcomes. Encourage consumers to identify special characteristics they valued, how your product or service solved their difficulties, and the positive influence it had on their business or personal lives. Detailed testimonials are more persuasive as they provide real evidence of usefulness.

Showcasing Diverse Customer Experiences: Collect testimonials from a diverse variety of consumers to highlight the broad appeal and versatility of your product or service. This diversity can encompass varied industries, company sizes, geographic regions, and use cases. Highlighting varied experiences can resonate with a wider audience and illustrate that your solution is effective across different circumstances.

Using Multimedia Testimonials: While textual testimonials are valuable, including multimedia features like video testimonials can be even more effective. Videos give a personal touch and allow potential consumers to see and hear from genuine people, making the testimonials more personable and credible. High-quality video testimonials can considerably enhance your marketing efforts.

Prominently Displaying Testimonials: Incorporate testimonials into your marketing materials, such as your website, social media profiles, email campaigns, and brochures. Highlight them on product pages, landing pages, and at critical points along the client journey. Prominently displaying testimonials ensures that potential clients receive favorable feedback at multiple touchpoints.

Creating Compelling Case Studies.

Case studies are thorough explanations of how your product or service helped specific clients achieve their objectives. They provide detailed insights while demonstrating your experience and capacity to generate results.

Selecting Relevant Success Stories: Choose case studies that are relevant to your intended audience. Concentrate on success stories that illustrate the issues, solutions, and outcomes that are most likely to appeal to potential customers. The more relatable and relevant the case study, the more compelling it will be.

A convincing case study should have a defined framework that includes an introduction to the customer, a discussion of the issues they faced, the solution offered by your product or service, and the results attained. Use subheadings, bullet points, and images to make the text easier to read and understand.

Quantitative and qualitative data should be combined to generate a well-rounded case study. Quantitative data provides objective evidence of achievement, whereas qualitative insights provide a human factor and help potential buyers connect with the tale.

Using Visuals and Graphics: Include visuals and graphics in your case studies, such as before-and-after images, charts, graphs, and infographics. Visual features can serve to clarify crucial points, make complicated information more accessible, and boost engagement. High-quality pictures can also help your case studies appear more appealing and professional.

Highlighting the Customer's Voice: Allow your customers to talk for themselves by presenting direct quotes and testimonials in the case studies. Their natural voices lend authenticity and make the story more appealing. Ensure that the customer's perspective is prominently displayed throughout the case study.

To increase the reach of your case studies, distribute them across multiple media. Publish them on your website, include them in email newsletters, promote them on social media, and include them into sales presentations. Consider producing downloadable PDFs for convenient sharing and offline use.

Creating an Online Presence

Using Social Media to Increase Trust

In today's digital landscape, establishing a strong online presence is critical for developing trust and engaging with clients. Social media networks provide excellent opportunity to communicate with your target audience, distribute useful content, and demonstrate your credibility.

Choosing the Right sites: Concentrate on the social media sites that are most popular among your target demographic. LinkedIn is best for B2B interactions, whereas Facebook, Instagram, and Twitter are great for B2C engagement. By selecting the appropriate platforms, you can ensure that your efforts reach the proper people.

Consistency and sincerity are essential for developing trust on social media. Regularly share high-quality material that fits your brand's beliefs and tone. Share a variety of promotional content, instructive posts, behind-the-scenes glimpses, and client testimonials. Creating authentic content that connects with your target audience might help you establish a devoted following.

Engage with Your Audience: Social media is a two-way communication channel. Respond to comments, mails, and mentions to keep your audience engaged. Express gratitude for favorable feedback and respond to any concerns or inquiries swiftly and professionally. Active participation shows that you care about your consumers and are dedicated to their pleasure.

Displaying User-Generated Content: Encourage customers to post about their experiences with your product or service on social media. User-generated content, such as images, reviews, and testimonials, can be an effective source of social proof. Share and highlight this information on your profiles to demonstrate real-world use and client satisfaction.

Hosting Live Sessions and Webinars: These are great ways to communicate with your audience in real time. Use these opportunities to give useful information, display products, answer questions, and interact with customers directly. Live conversations can help you create trust and knowledge in your sector.

Collaborating with Influencers: Working with influencers who have a large following in your field can help you expand your reach and reputation. Influencers can promote your product, discuss their experiences, and produce content to emphasize your brand. Choose influencers whose ideals are consistent with your company and who can truly advocate for your goods.

Engaging with Customers Online

Engagement with clients online extends beyond social media. It entails using numerous digital platforms to develop meaningful interactions and long-lasting partnerships.

Email Marketing Campaigns: Email marketing is still an effective technique for client involvement. Send out targeted emails with value, such as newsletters, product updates, special offers, and instructional content. Segment your email list so that your messages are tailored to different customer groups and remain relevant.

Create and cultivate online communities where customers may connect, share their experiences, and support one another. This could happen via forums, social media groups, or specific community platforms. Active participation in these groups fosters a sense of belonging and loyalty in your customers.

Material marketing entails creating and sharing useful material that addresses the requirements and interests of your target audience. This may include blog posts, articles, videos, podcasts, and infographics. High-quality content establishes you as an expert in your sector and offers continual value to your clients, keeping them interested in your business.

Webinars and Virtual Events: Use webinars and virtual events to connect with customers in a more interactive way. These events can include a wide range of topics, including product demonstrations, training sessions, industry insights, and customer success stories. Virtual events allow for real-time interaction and knowledge transfer.

Online surveys and feedback forms can help you obtain insights from your clients. Understand their requirements, preferences, and level of satisfaction. Use this input to improve your products, services, and customer experience. Showing that you value and act on customer input builds trust in your brand.

Exceptional Customer Support: Make sure your online customer service is responsive, friendly, and easily accessible. Provide several methods of help, such as live chat, email, and social media. Provide prompt and effective solutions to customer concerns, and follow up to assure their satisfaction. Exceptional support fosters trust and demonstrates your dedication to client service.

Using social proof like as testimonials, case studies, and a strong internet presence is critical for establishing trust and credibility in sales. Collecting and leveraging client testimonials, developing engaging case studies, and properly displaying them can have a substantial impact on potential consumers' purchasing decisions. Creating an online presence through consistent and authentic social media participation, user-generated content, and influencer collaborations expands your reach and credibility. Engaging with customers through email marketing, content marketing, online communities, webinars, surveys, and great customer service ensures that value is delivered on a continuous basis and develops lasting relationships. Sales professionals may create trust, increase client happiness, and generate long-term success by employing social proof successfully and remaining engaged online.

Chapter 7: Ethical Selling Practices

Maintaining ethical standards in the competitive world of sales is critical not only for long-term success, but also for creating and retaining client trust. Ethical sales methods ensure that relationships with clients are built on honesty, integrity, and respect. This chapter discusses the significance of avoiding deceptive approaches, encouraging ethical persuasion, and guaranteeing openness in pricing and policies.

Avoid Manipulative Tactics.

Ethical Persuasion vs. Manipulation

The contrast between ethical persuasion and manipulation is crucial in sales. Ethical persuasion entails convincing clients using honest, transparent information and real intent, whereas manipulation use deceptive or forceful approaches to close a deal.

Understanding Ethical Persuasion: Ethical persuasion is around providing clients with accurate and relevant information that allows them to make educated judgments. This approach respects the customer's autonomy and the right to select freely. Ethical salespeople prioritize understanding the customer's needs and delivering solutions that truly meet those needs.

The Role of Integrity: Integrity is essential for ethical persuasion. Salespeople must guarantee that any assertions about their products or services are accurate and supported. Misleading information or inflating benefits can result in short-term profits but will eventually harm trust and reputation.

Building Trust Through Honesty: Honesty is the foundation of ethical selling techniques. Being open about a product's strengths, potential disadvantages, and limitations promotes credibility. Customers value honesty and are more inclined to trust and stick with a salesperson who is forthright and transparent.

Focusing on Long-Term Relationships: Ethical persuasion prioritizes long-term relationships over immediate advantages. Salespeople should prioritize customer happiness and long-term loyalty over quick sales. This method promotes a solid, trusting relationship, which can lead to repeat business and referrals.

Respecting Customer Autonomy: Ethical sales methods acknowledge the customer's right to make their own choices. This includes avoiding high-pressure sales tactics, respecting the customer's decision-making process, and providing them enough space and time to examine their options. Respecting autonomy promotes trust and a great client experience.

Avoid Manipulative Tactics.

Manipulative practices erode confidence and harm the reputations of both the salesperson and the organization. Avoiding these strategies is critical for sustaining ethical sales practices.

High-Pressure Sales Tactics: High-pressure tactics involve instilling a sense of urgency or anxiety in consumers in order to persuade them to make hasty decisions. These approaches might cause buyer's remorse and weaken confidence. Ethical salespeople provide consumers the knowledge they need and the time they need to make informed selections without feeling rushed.

False scarcity is a deceitful strategy that involves stating limited supply when this is not the case. While actual scarcity can be an effective sales approach, fraudulently saying that a product is in short supply in order to push people into a purchase is unethical.

Misleading Information: Giving false information about a product's features, benefits, or performance is manipulation. Ethical sales professionals guarantee that all information supplied is accurate and verified. Misleading customers not only undermines trust but can also lead to legal ramifications.

Omitting Important Information: Withholding essential information that could affect a customer's decision is another sort of manipulation. Salespeople should present a thorough and fair assessment of the product, including any potential downsides or limits.

Emotional Manipulation: Using emotional manipulation to exploit a customer's vulnerabilities or anxieties is unethical.

Ethical persuasion requires identifying and addressing genuine client wants and concerns without manipulating emotions unfairly.

Transparency in Pricing and Policies

Transparency in pricing and policies is essential for ethical sales. Clear and honest information about pricing structures, return policies, and refunds promotes trust and a great customer experience.

Clear Pricing Structures

Transparent pricing structures allow clients to understand exactly what they are paying for and why. This clarity reduces uncertainty and increases trust.

Breakdown of expenses: Giving clients a full breakdown of expenses, including any additional fees or charges, helps them grasp the entire price. Transparency about what is included in the price and any potential additional charges (such as shipping, installation, and maintenance) eliminates surprises.

Consistent Pricing: Pricing that is consistent across all channels and for all customers helps to avoid misunderstanding and perceived unfairness. Ensure that listed prices reflect what customers pay, and that any discounts or specials are clearly conveyed.

Avoiding Hidden costs: Hidden costs are a typical cause of customer unhappiness. Ethical sales methods include providing all potential fees upfront, so that buyers understand the overall cost before making a purchase.

Clarity in Discounts and Promotions: Make sure you disclose the terms and limitations of any discounts or promotions. Customers should understand the eligibility requirements, length, and any limitations that come with special offers.

Transparent Financing alternatives: When providing financing alternatives, be upfront about interest rates, repayment terms, and any associated expenses. Customers should completely comprehend their financial commitment.

Transparent Return and Refund Policies

Clear and fair return and refund procedures are critical to establishing customer trust. These rules should be simple to comprehend and accessible, giving customers confidence in their purchase decisions.

Easy Access to Policies: Make sure return and refund policies are easily accessible on your website, in-store, and in all marketing materials. Customers should not have to conduct extensive searches to find this information.

Write return and refund policies in plain and simple terms. Avoid using legal jargon, as this can confuse customers. The policy should specify the procedure for returns and refunds, including any criteria or time constraints.

Fair and Reasonable Terms: Set up fair and reasonable return and refund policies. Customers should feel confident that their rights are respected and that they can return a product if it does not match their expectations or has flaws.

Quick and Efficient Processing: Ensure that returns and refunds are handled quickly and efficiently. Delays or problems in the return procedure can cause consumer frustration and destroy trust. Streamlined processes improve client satisfaction.

Customer Support for Returns: Make it easy for customers to return items and receive refunds. Dedicated support channels, such as a hotline or email assistance, can help resolve issues quickly and provide a smooth experience for customers.

Returns and refunds provide an opportunity to obtain feedback and enhance your products and services. Understanding why customers return products can lead to significant insights for future improvements.

Chapter 8: Adapting To Different Personalities

In sales, one size does not fit all. Understanding and adjusting to various client personas is critical for establishing rapport and effectively serving their demands. This chapter delves into how to detect different personality types, change sales methods accordingly, and develop strong relationships with diverse consumers.

Understanding Customers' Personalities

Every consumer is unique, yet many share personality qualities that can be generically described. Understanding these characteristics enables salespeople to customize their approach to better connect with each customer.

Common Personality Types:

- **Analytical Customer:**

Characteristics: Detail-oriented, systematic, and data-driven. Analytical buyers want to know all of the facts and numbers before making a decision.

Approach: Provide comprehensive information, such as data, statistics, and evidence. Be prepared to answer thorough questions and back up your arguments with verifiable evidence. Avoid hurrying them; they require time to assimilate information.

- **The Amiable Customer:**

Characteristics: Friendly, cooperative, and relationship-focused. Amiable clients respect personal ties and prefer to work with someone they can trust.

Approach: Establish a personal connection by expressing genuine interest in their wants and problems. Maintain a pleasant, empathic tone and avoid aggressive sales approaches. Highlight how your product or service will benefit them in a positive way.

- **The Expressive Customers:**

Characteristics: enthusiastic, outgoing, and creative. Expressive clients are motivated by emotions and personal experiences.

Approach: Give them an active and exciting presentation. Use narrative to demonstrate how your product or service will improve their lives. Be friendly and enthusiastic about what you're selling.

- **The Driver Customer:**

Goal-oriented, determined, and outspoken. Drivers prioritize outcomes and efficiency.

Approach: Be straightforward and to the point. Emphasize the actual advantages and ROI of your product or service. Respect their time by remaining concise and prepared. Show how your solution connects with their aims and objectives.

Adapting Sales Strategies for Different Personality Types

Tailoring your sales technique to your customer's personality type will help you sell more effectively. Here are some techniques for adapting to each type:

- **Analytical Customers**

Provide detailed information: Analytical customers value completeness. Provide them with precise product details, performance data, and comparisons to competitors. Written materials, brochures, and whitepapers can be very useful.

Be Ready to Answer inquiries: Expect and welcome a lot of inquiries. Be patient and offer straightforward, evidence-based responses. Show that you are educated and trustworthy by being open about your product's benefits and limits.

Use Logic and Data: Emphasize logical reasoning and quantitative benefits. Case studies, testimonials, and empirical proof can all help to demonstrate the value of your product.

Give Them Time: Analytical customers require time to analyze their alternatives. Don't press them to make a rapid decision. Follow up with more information and be available to answer any questions they may have.

- **Friendly customers**

Build a Relationship: Spend time getting to know friendly consumers. Inquire about their preferences, wants, and concerns. Demonstrate empathy and compassion, and make them feel valuable and respected.

Use a Personal Touch: Personalize your communication and demonstrate real concern for their well-being. Share success stories from other consumers who have used your product, emphasizing the helpful elements of your service.

Be Patient and Supportive: Friendly clients may take longer to make a selection since they want comfort and consensus.

Be patient and sympathetic, offering encouragement and responding to any worries they may have.

Highlight Customer assistance: Emphasize your company's great customer assistance and after-sales service. Assure customers that they will receive constant support throughout their experience with your product.

- **Customers who are open and expressive**

Engage Their Emotions: Build emotional connections with expressive customers. Use colorful descriptions and compelling stories to demonstrate the impact of your product. Demonstrate enthusiasm and passion for what you are offering.

Be Energetic and Enthusiastic: Match their enthusiasm. Expressive customers value dynamic and engaging relationships. Make sure your lectures are dynamic and entertaining.

Highlight your product's amazing and transformative benefits. Use testimonials and success stories to demonstrate how other people have benefited in interesting and positive ways.

Create a Personal Connection: Be nice and approachable in order to establish a personal relationship. Expressive clients respect relationships and are more likely to trust someone with whom they have a connection.

- **Driver Customers**

Be Direct and Efficient: Respect the driver's time by being direct and concise. Provide clear information, emphasizing the primary benefits and ROI of your product. Avoid chit conversation and get right to the topic.

Demonstrate Value: Explain how your product can help them reach their objectives swiftly and efficiently. Use metrics, performance statistics, and case studies to demonstrate actual advantages and outcomes.

Respect Their Authority: Recognize their competence and authority. Allow them to dominate the discourse and make decisions. Provide instruction and support, but allow them to lead the way.

Be Prepared and Organized: Drivers value preparation and organization. Make sure your presentation is well-structured and that you have all of the required material available.

Establishing Rapport with Various Customer Types

Developing rapport is critical for developing trust and cultivating long-term connections. Here are some general tactics for developing rapport with various client personalities:

Active Listening: Regardless of personality type, active listening is essential for developing rapport. Pay attention to the customer's words, acknowledge their problems, and answer carefully. Demonstrate that you value their feedback and are really concerned with satisfying their requirements.

Adapt Your Communication Style: Tailor your communication style to the customer's personality. Use the language, tone, and pace that people are accustomed to. Mirroring their communication style can help to establish a connection and make them feel understood.

Empathy: Acknowledge the customer's sentiments and worries. Understanding their point of view and demonstrating that you care about their experience might help enhance your relationship.

Be authentic: Authenticity is essential for developing trust. Be sincere in your dealings and avoid a rehearsed or too polished tone. Customers value sincerity and are more likely to trust those who are honest and direct.

Follow Through: Consistency and dependability are essential for developing rapport. Deliver on your pledges and obligations. Ensure that you follow through on what you've discussed and offer any further assistance or information as needed.

Personalize Your Approach: Tailor your sales pitch to each unique customer's demands and preferences. Demonstrate that you've taken the time to understand their unique issue and are providing a solution that is tailored to them.

Conclusion

Building trust in sales is more than a technique; it is a fundamental principle that supports successful, long-term commercial relationships. We've covered many aspects of trust-building in this book, from personal credibility and efficient communication to keeping commitments and adjusting to varied consumer types. The ultimate goal is to establish long-term relationships that extend beyond the initial transaction, ensuring client loyalty and satisfaction.

The path begins with developing personal credibility. Salespeople must develop self-awareness and honesty, exhibiting authenticity in all interactions. Personal integrity is the foundation of trust; without it, even the most sophisticated sales strategies fall short. Professionalism and continuous learning increase credibility by demonstrating to customers that you are not just trustworthy but also a qualified expert in your industry. Sharing knowledge without overselling fosters a balanced, respectful connection that puts the customer's best interests first.

Trust is also built on effective communication. Active listening entails truly understanding the customer's requirements and problems, which promotes a sense of respect and affirmation. Clear and transparent communication fosters trust by being honest about products or services and setting reasonable expectations. Customers value honesty and clarity, which helps to avoid misunderstandings and potential disappointments.

Delivering on promises is crucial. Consistency and dependability are crucial characteristics for any successful salesperson. Meeting deadlines, following through on pledges, and resolving difficulties quickly and effectively demonstrate a strong commitment to client satisfaction. When clients understand that they can rely on you, their confidence in your brand develops.

Building long-term relationships extends beyond the initial sale. Providing value to clients through ongoing support, regular follow-ups, and keeping touch demonstrates your commitment to their success. Excellent customer service, which includes providing memorable experiences and constructively managing concerns, builds trust and encourages return business.

Using social evidence is an effective strategy for establishing trust. Testimonials and case studies provide real-world evidence of the benefits of your product or service, allowing potential customers to make more confident purchasing decisions. An active online presence, particularly on social media, allows for ongoing engagement and conversation, reinforcing your reputation as a trustworthy and responsive organization.

Ethical sales tactics are crucial. Avoiding deceptive tactics and preserving transparency in pricing and policy safeguards the integrity of your consumer interactions. By stressing ethical persuasion over manipulation and being open about costs and return policies, you demonstrate that your company appreciates honesty and fairness.

Finally, successful sales require the ability to adapt to varied personalities. Understanding and appreciating the various ways clients think and make decisions enables you to adjust your approach, resulting in stronger, more personal interactions. Recognizing and adjusting to different personality types allows you to communicate more effectively and suit each customer's specific needs.

The principles discussed in this book give a complete foundation for establishing trust and attaining sales results. Trust is the foundation of any meaningful business connection. By focusing on personal credibility, effective communication, consistent delivery, long-term relationship building, leveraging social proof, ethical sales practices, and adapting to customer personalities, you can lay the groundwork for long-term growth and customer loyalty. In an ever-changing environment, these timeless concepts will remain critical for anybody trying to succeed in the sales industry.

www.ingramcontent.com/pod-product-compliance
Lightning Source LLC
Chambersburg PA
CBHW071839210526
45479CB00001B/211